reverence

VIRTUES OF MY HEART

Written and Illustrated by Melissa López Charepoo

Text and Illustrations
©2023 Melissa López Charepoo

First published 2023. Reprint 2026.

ISBN 978-1-971750-27-9 (paperback)

To all who make the world a better place by striving for reverence in their daily lives.

Have you ever wondered what it means to be **reverent**?

Reverence is having a deep respect for our Creator and being aware that we are always in His presence. Being reverent makes our hearts joyful and helps us develop many other virtues as well. We show reverence when we feel we are in the presence of something bigger than ourselves, like when we pray to God. We also show **reverence** by having a deep respect for God's creation.

We can strive to show **reverence** in many ways of our lives!

I strive to be reverent by having the **self-discipline** of praying every day. To pray, I sit in a quiet space, then I close my eyes and say a prayer from the heart or read a prayer in a melodious voice. As I pray, I'm grateful to my Creator for everything and ask for guidance in difficult times. I also reflect on my actions and think of the things I did right and the things I have to improve. Having the **self-discipline** of praying every day helps me fulfill my purpose in life.

How do you strive for reverence by practicing **self-discipline** to pray every day?

As a family, we strive for reverence by praying together. I help us build bonds of **unity** when we worship our Creator as a family. When we are praying together, everyone listens carefully and thinks of the words being said as each one of us takes our turn to pray. We also like to sing prayers or play soft music to accompany them. Our prayers are hopeful in difficult times and joyful in good times. Praying together brings our hearts closer.

How do you create **unity** in your family by striving for reverence?

In my community there are many places of worship, like churches, synagogues, temples, and mosques. These places are sacred because we can feel the presence of our Creator in our hearts in a special way. Activities in places of worship may vary, but usually they are serene and full of prayers and meditation. When we visit a sacred place of worship, we show reverence by dressing modestly, acting calmly, and speaking softly, as we are aware that many other people are coming together to worship our Creator as well. Our hearts are **joyful** and our **faith** in God increases when we come together as a community to worship our Creator.

What is your place of worship? How do you show reverence in your place of worship? What activities in your place of worship make your **faith** toward our Creator stronger?

At school, I strive for reverence to our Creator by **serving** others. I always feel closer to our Creator when I'm useful to someone in need. Whether helping the teacher clean up our classroom after a busy day or helping a friend with a question, I'm always joyful to serve others without expecting anything in return.

How do you show reverence to our Creator by **serving** others in need?

In our free time, we love to do nature walks as a family. Nature makes us feel so small in comparison of how big the whole creation is. It helps us recognize that there is a creative force larger than us. We feel reverence for our Creator when we admire in **awe** how beautiful and perfect His creation is. We always feel the presence of God when we are in nature.

What is your favorite spot to visit in nature? How does being in **awe** of nature increase your reverence for our Creator?

In my daily life, I strive for reverence for our Creator by treating all living things with **honor** and **nobility**. All living things, but especially human beings, deserve to be treated with **honor**, a deep respect because they have been created noble, born as spiritual beings. I strive to treat everyone with respect and kindness.

How do you show reverence to our Creator by treating all living things with **honor** and **nobility**?

As citizens of a country, we show reverence to our Creator by striving to **respect** the laws of our country and our national symbols. Laws give us rights, which are our privileges; and responsibilities, which are the things that we need to do. National symbols represent what our country hopes to be. We also understand that some laws are not fair, and that is why we are called to work together to make them more just. Our Creator wants us to live in an orderly and caring world, and by consulting and understanding, we can create laws that are **fair**, safe, and **loving** for everyone.

What are some laws in your country? Which laws in your country do you think could be improved to make them **fair** and just for everyone?

As caretakers of the world, we show reverence to our Creator when we are **responsible** for our planet. We can be **responsible** with our planet in so many ways, like picking up the trash at the beach or planting a tree. It is our **responsibility** to take care of our planet in any way we can, so that many others can enjoy this beautiful place that we call home.

How do you show reverence to our Creator by being **responsible** with our planet?

As you can see, we can strive to be **reverent** to our Creator anywhere we are.
By being reverent, our hearts develop many other virtues, such as self-discipline,
unity, faith, service, awe, honor and nobility, respect, and responsibility.

Our hearts will always be joyful when we strive to be reverent to our Creator in
everything we do!

Glossary

Awe – a feeling of reverence, deep respect, humility

Faith – having deep trust in our Creator

Honor – to regard with great respect and admiration

Nobility – understanding that all human beings were created spiritual beings

Respect – a deep admiration for someone or something

Responsibility – sense of duty; being accountable for our choices

Reverence – deep respect for someone or something

Sacred – something that connects us with our Creator; something created for religious purposes

Self-discipline – being able to control our actions

Service – the act of helping others without expecting anything in return

Unity – being part of a whole; togetherness

References:

The Virtues Project Cards

Oxford English Dictionary

Heartfelt thanks to:

My beloved husband Darioush Charepoo for all his support.

Our dearly loved boys for being the inspiration.

Leanna Guillén Mora for helping with proofreading and editing the book.